S0-BTD-006

CAVE LIFE

PHOTOGRAPHED BY
FRANK GREENAWAY

WRITTEN BY
CHRISTIANE GUNZI

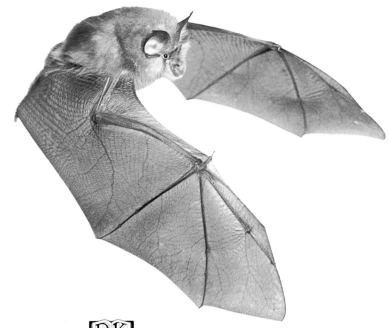

A Dorling Kindersley Book

DK

Dorling Kindersley
LONDON, NEW YORK, SYDNEY, DELHI
PARIS, MUNICH, JOHANNESBURG

Editor Deborah Murrell   **Art editor** Val Wright
Senior editor Christiane Gunzi   **Designer** Floyd Sayers
Design assistants Nicola Rawson, Will Wood
Production Louise Barratt
Illustrations Nick Hall
Index Jane Parker
Managing editor Sophie Mitchell
Managing art editor Miranda Kennedy
U.S. editor B. Alison Weir

Consultants
Dave Clarke, Theresa Greenaway,
Gordon Howes, Mark O'Shea, Matthew Robertson,
Vicky Silverton, Edward Wade, Kathie Way

With thanks to Sue Dewar, Judith Marshall, and Mark O'Shea for
supplying some of the animals and information in this book.

First American Edition, 1993
Paperback Edition, 2000
2 4 6 8 10 9 7 5 3 1

Published in the United States by
Dorling Kindersley Publishing, Inc., 95 Madison Avenue, New York, New York 10016

Copyright © 1993 Dorling Kindersley Ltd.

Library of Congress Cataloging-in-Publication Data
Gunzi, Christiane.
Cave Life/Christiane Gunzi ; photography by Frank Greenaway.–
1st American ed.
p.   cm. – (Look closer)
Includes index.
Summary: Discusses the plants and animals that live in caves.
Includes the peacock butterfly, cave cricket, and Natterer's bat.
ISBN 0-7894-6100-5
1. Cave fauna–Juvenile literature. 2. Cave plants–Juvenile literature.
[1. Cave animals. 2. Cave plants.]
I. Greenaway, Frank, ill. II. Title. III. Series.
QH89.G86 1993
574.909'44–dc20
92-53490-CIP-AC

Color reproduction by Colourscan, Singapore
Printed and bound in China by L. Rex Printing Co., Ltd

For our complete catalog visit
www.dk.com

CONTENTS

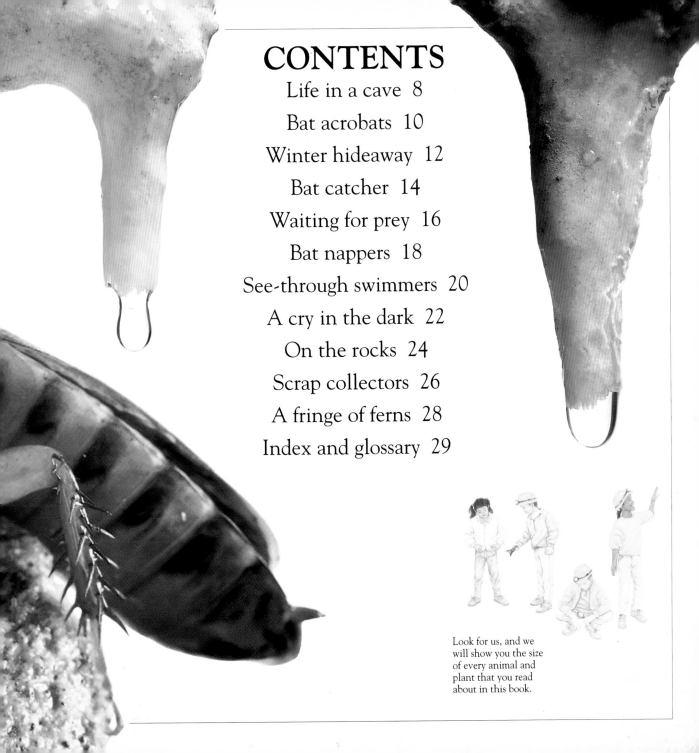

Look for us, and we will show you the size of every animal and plant that you read about in this book.

LIFE IN A CAVE

A CAVE CAN TAKE THOUSANDS of years to form. Most caves are found in limestone rock. As rain falls, carbon dioxide from the air turns it into a weak acid, which dissolves the rock. Over the years, the acid makes a hollow, which grows and grows, until finally a cave is formed. Large caves are called caverns. They may stretch for many miles, and often contain lakes and streams. The temperature in a cave hardly changes throughout the year, and there is usually no light at all. Many cave animals have lost the use of their eyes because they do not need them in the dark. They often have a strong sense of touch instead, to help them feel their way. Bats, insects, birds, amphibians, and fish have all adapted to living in caves, and many other kinds of animals spend part of the year sheltering there.

The Natterer's bat's
(Myotis nattereri)
body is 2 in. long and it has a wingspan of 11 in. It lives in North Africa, northern Europe, and southern Scandinavia.

The young hart's tongue fern's
(Phyllitis scolopendrium)
fronds are 4 in. long. It lives in Europe, Japan, North America, and western Asia.

The sea spleenwort's
(Asplenium marinum)
fronds are 5 in. long. It lives in North Africa and western Europe.

The maidenhair fern's
(Adiantum capillus-veneris)
fronds are 6 in. long. It lives all over the world.

The lesser horseshoe bat's
(Rhinolophus hipposiderus)
body is 1 1/2 in. long and it has a wingspan of 10 in. It lives in central Asia, central and southern Europe, and North Africa.

The barn owl
(Tyto alba)
is 9 1/2 in. high. It lives in Africa, Australia, northern Asia, southern Europe, the Americas, and the Middle East.

The young Surinam cockroach's
body is 1/2 in. long.

The peacock butterfly's
(*Inachis io*)
wingspan is 2 in.
It lives in Asia
and Europe.

The cave spider's
(*Meta menardi*)
body is 1/3 in. long.
It lives north of
the equator.

The African cave cricket's
(*Pholeogryllus geertsi*)
body is 1 in. long.
It lives in North Africa
and southern Europe.

The red-tailed racer's
(*Gonyosoma oxycephala*)
head is 1 in. long and its
body is 5 ft. long.
It lives in Southeast Asia.

The herald moth's
(*Scoliopteryx libatrix*)
wingspan is 11/2 in.
It lives in Asia,
Europe, and Japan.

The adult Surinam cockroach's
(*Pycnoscelis surinamensis*)
body is 3/4 in. long.
It lives in tropical areas
all over the world.

The blind cave characin
(*Astyanax mexicanus*)
is 11/2 in. long
It lives in Mexico.

BAT ACROBATS

HORSESHOE BATS ARE expert fliers, twisting and turning in midair as they chase after insects, such as moths. Like other bats, they leave their roost (the place where they live) at night to hunt for food. At dawn, they return to the roost and rest hanging upside down. Lesser horseshoe bats like these often live together in a large group called a colony. They mate in autumn, but the females do not give birth until the following summer, when the weather is warm and there is plenty of food to eat. Each female has one young. The young feed on their mothers' milk for up to six weeks, until they are strong enough to fly. Then they follow their mothers out of the cave at night to learn to hunt. These bats may live for as long as 20 years.

The wings wrap around the body like a cloak when the bat is resting. They help keep in moisture, which keeps the bat from drying out.

NOISY NOSTRILS
Some kinds of bats have extraordinary noses with decorative flaps on them, called nose-leaves. The horseshoe shape of this bat's nose-leaf gives it its name. Nose-leaves are useful as well as decorative. They help bats direct the ultrasounds that they send out through their nostrils.

The bat's body is covered in fur, which helps keep it warm.

GUESS WHAT?
Bats form a group of animals called *Chiroptera*, which means "hand flappers." This is a good name because a bat flies by flapping the long, webbed fingers that are part of its wings.

The eyes are small, but these bats can see quite well.

The round shape of this nose-leaf helps the bat send out ultrasounds.

NURSERY TIME
Female lesser horseshoe bats often gather in a cave or building to give birth, forming a nursery that may consist of 200 or 300 bats. Colonies may use the same nursery for hundreds of years. A newborn bat has no fur, and its eyes do not open for about ten days. But it begins to suckle its mother's milk just a few minutes after birth. At night, when the adult females return from hunting, each finds her own baby among all the others by its individual smell and voice.

Each wing consists of elastic, leathery skin, supported by the arm, leg, and finger bones.

MAKING ECHOES
Bats find their prey in the dark by sending out high-pitched squeaks. When the sounds bounce off an object, such as a flying insect, the bat can hear the echo. This is called echolocation, because the echo helps the bat locate (find) its prey. Sounds like these, which are too high-pitched for people to hear, are called ultrasounds. Some kinds of moths can hear ultrasounds, and this enables them to escape from a bat.

The clawed toes
are useful for
gripping rocks.

GNAT SNATCHER
Horseshoe bats are insectivores (insect
eaters), with large ears that help them
detect their prey in the dark. As they
hunt, they swoop close to the
ground to snatch up beetles, gnats,
and spiders, as well as moths.
They can also hover in midair.
On cold, wet evenings, when
there are few insects to
catch, bats usually prefer to
stay dry in their roost.

NEXT-DOOR NEIGHBORS
In winter, colonies of up to 400 lesser
horseshoe bats may hibernate in one
cave. But they do not hang too close
together; they always leave a little
space. These bats can hardly walk
at all, but their legs are perfectly
adapted for hanging upside down.
If a lesser horseshoe bat dies
during hibernation, its body
may stay hanging in exactly
the same position for
many years.

The ears are
large and pointed,
and each one can
turn separately.

Whiskers help the
bat feel when an
insect is near
enough to be
snapped up.

WINTER HIDEAWAY

FROM EARLY AUTUMN right through the winter months, herald moths hibernate in dark caves, hollow trees, and old buildings. In early spring, they awake and search for a mate. Female herald moths lay their eggs on the leaves of willow, poplar, and sallow trees. The eggs hatch into long, green caterpillars that feed greedily on the leaves. After about two months, they spin cocoons and change into pupae. In summer, an adult moth emerges from each cocoon. The adults only live until the following spring, just long enough to mate and lay eggs. Herald moths are nocturnal (active at night). They rest in dark places during the day, with their back wings folded under their front wings. At night, they feed on nectar from tree blossoms and flowers.

A moth's body is furry. This helps keep it warm during the night, when it is active.

These butterflies have strong wings, making them powerful fliers.

These eyespots on the wings frighten off enemies.

The wings are covered with tiny, colored scales that overlap each other.

SPRING FEEDERS

Peacock butterflies awake on the first warm days of spring to feed on wild flowers, and to mate and lay their eggs. The females lay clusters of eggs on stinging nettle plants. Black, spiky caterpillars hatch out and feed on the nettle leaves for two to three months, then turn into pupae. Adult butterflies emerge in summer, to eat as much as they can before finding a dark place, such as a cave, to hibernate in.

FLASHING EYES

A peacock butterfly is difficult to spot during hibernation because it usually rests with its wings closed, and the undersides are dull in color. But if this butterfly is disturbed, it flutters its wings, revealing two large eyespots. At the same time, it rubs its front and back wings together, which makes a hissing sound to frighten off the intruder.

There are claws at the end of each leg for gripping on to rocks and other surfaces.

During hibernation, the peacock butterfly rolls its antennae up out of the way.

GUESS WHAT?

Moths hold their wings out flat when they are resting, while butterflies rest with their wings together. This is an easy way to tell the difference between a moth and a butterfly.

LONG-DISTANCE ROMANCE
Male herald moths have very sensitive antennae that can detect scents. During the breeding season, the females produce a special chemical, called a pheromone, which attracts males for mating. A male herald moth can locate a female from up to a mile away.

LEAVE ME ALONE
This herald moth is the color and shape of a dead leaf. The patchy patterns on its wings help disguise it against the trees where it rests, so predators, such as birds, do not always notice it.

When the moth is resting, it looks like a leaf. This helps it avoid being eaten during hibernation.

BAT CATCHER

THE RED-TAILED RACER spends much of its time slithering among the branches of tropical forests. But it also likes to venture inside cool, dark caves. In and around a cave there are plenty of lizards, frogs, small birds, and bats to eat. A bat sleeping in its roost is easy prey for this snake as it glides silently over the rocks. Red-tailed racers mate during the rainy season. About a month later, the female finds somewhere warm and moist to lay her eggs, such as inside a rotten log or under leaf litter. She usually lays between five and twelve eggs, then leaves them. After six weeks or so, depending on the surrounding temperature, the young hatch out and each one wriggles away by itself to find shelter and food.

GUESS WHAT?
This snake gets its name from its reddish brown tail. Red-tailed racers are not venomous (poisonous), so they are not dangerous to humans. Even so, they can give a painful bite.

This snake has inflated a special lung inside its body to make itself appear bigger.

The snake can hold the front part of its body out horizontally to catch prey.

The tail is wrapped around a rock, and acts like an anchor to give the snake a firm grip.

The mouth can open very wide to snatch bats and birds as they fly past.

The scales on the underside are wide and strong.

RACING REPTILE
Red-tailed racers move very quickly, and they are extremely agile. Their slender body shape enables them to slide easily between rocks and through undergrowth. Most snakes have a cylindrical (tube-shaped) body. But the underside of a red-tailed racer is flattened, with quite sharp edges. This helps the snake to hang on when it is climbing up trees or over rocks.

AN EASY MEAL

The red-tailed racer sometimes hangs around the cave entrance with its mouth wide open, waiting for bats to come out to feed. As the bats fly out in hundreds, the snake grabs the first one to brush against its head. It holds the bat firmly with its teeth, and coils itself around it to constrict (squeeze) and suffocate it. Each meal takes a long time to digest, so the snake only eats once or twice a month.

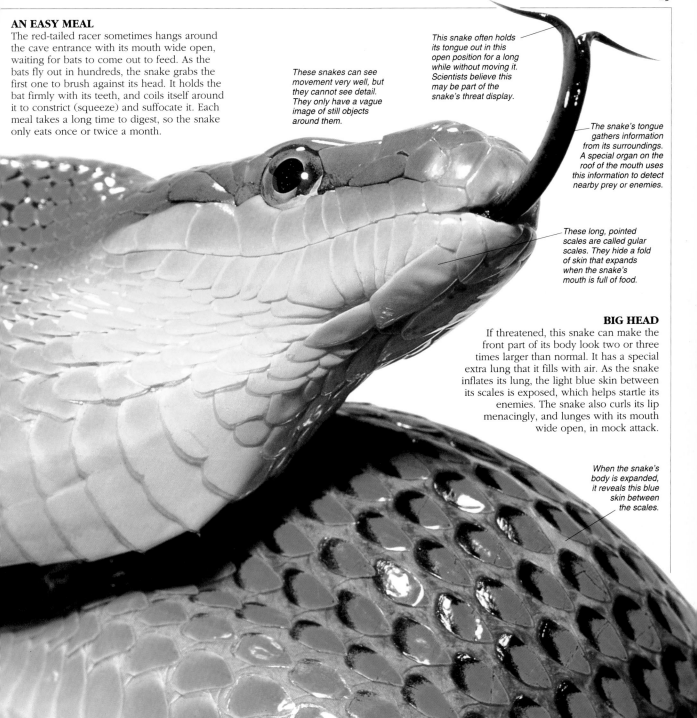

These snakes can see movement very well, but they cannot see detail. They only have a vague image of still objects around them.

This snake often holds its tongue out in this open position for a long while without moving it. Scientists believe this may be part of the snake's threat display.

The snake's tongue gathers information from its surroundings. A special organ on the roof of the mouth uses this information to detect nearby prey or enemies.

These long, pointed scales are called gular scales. They hide a fold of skin that expands when the snake's mouth is full of food.

BIG HEAD

If threatened, this snake can make the front part of its body look two or three times larger than normal. It has a special extra lung that it fills with air. As the snake inflates its lung, the light blue skin between its scales is exposed, which helps startle its enemies. The snake also curls its lip menacingly, and lunges with its mouth wide open, in mock attack.

When the snake's body is expanded, it reveals this blue skin between the scales.

WAITING FOR PREY

NEAR THE ENTRANCE to the cave, little cave spiders wait to trap unsuspecting insects on their silken webs. They are usually found less than 16 yards inside the cave, because there is more prey to catch close to the opening. Like all spiders, these creatures are carnivores (meat eaters). They feed mainly on flies and moths, but they also like to eat millipedes and cockroaches. In summer, each female spins a sac of silk and lays her eggs inside it. Then she seals the sac with more silk to protect the eggs. The following spring, young spiderlings hatch out of their eggs. At first the spiderlings have no claws or hairs, and they cannot eat. They stay inside the safety of the egg sac for up to a day, until they have molted (shed) their skin for the first time. Then they cut their way out of the sac and begin to fend for themselves.

The spider fixes its egg sac to the rock with four short threads that act like an anchor.

This thread looks like a single strand, but it may be made of many strands of silk.

The spider's head and thorax are joined, forming the cephalothorax.

The narrow part that joins the cephalothorax to the abdomen is called the pedicel.

DEADLY JAB
A spider's jaws have sharp fangs for biting prey. Near the end of each fang, there is a tiny hole that is connected to poison sacs. When the spider bites its victim, it injects poison through each hole to paralyze the prey.

SACS OF SILK
Spiders spin different sorts of silk for different jobs, such as wrapping up prey, or making the egg sac. Cave spiders spin very large egg sacs, which they hang from the ceiling of the cave on long, thin threads. Predators moving around on the ceiling do not always notice the sacs hanging below them.

GUESS WHAT?
Many spiders do not live long enough to see their young hatch. But these cave spiders can live for several years. The females guard their young fiercely, and will attack anything that threatens them.

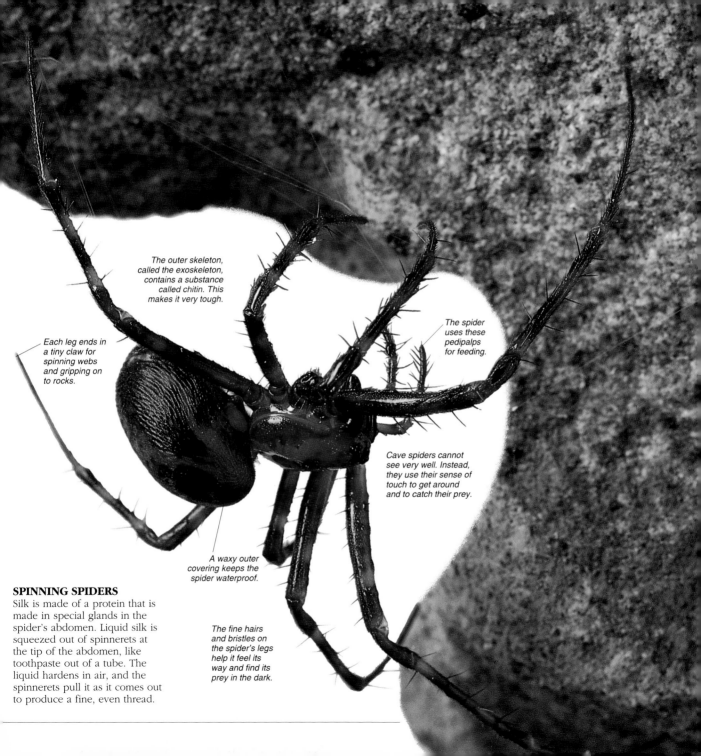

The outer skeleton, called the exoskeleton, contains a substance called chitin. This makes it very tough.

The spider uses these pedipalps for feeding.

Each leg ends in a tiny claw for spinning webs and gripping on to rocks.

Cave spiders cannot see very well. Instead, they use their sense of touch to get around and to catch their prey.

A waxy outer covering keeps the spider waterproof.

SPINNING SPIDERS

Silk is made of a protein that is made in special glands in the spider's abdomen. Liquid silk is squeezed out of spinnerets at the tip of the abdomen, like toothpaste out of a tube. The liquid hardens in air, and the spinnerets pull it as it comes out to produce a fine, even thread.

The fine hairs and bristles on the spider's legs help it feel its way and find its prey in the dark.

BAT NAPPERS

IN EARLY WINTER, Natterer's bats begin their hibernation. They often fly back to a cave that they have used before. These tiny mammals can squeeze themselves into the smallest cracks and crevices in the roof of a cave. Sometimes they sleep under rocks on the cave floor. But on the ground they are in more danger from predators, such as rats and foxes. In summer, female bats group together to give birth to one young each in a hollow tree or in the roof of a building. This is called a nursery, and the females care for the young there until they can fly. Natterer's bats are skillful fliers, and they can hover, too. Young Natterer's bats soon learn to hunt like their mothers. They scoop up insects such as flies, beetles, and larvae, with their tails, then flick them into their mouths.

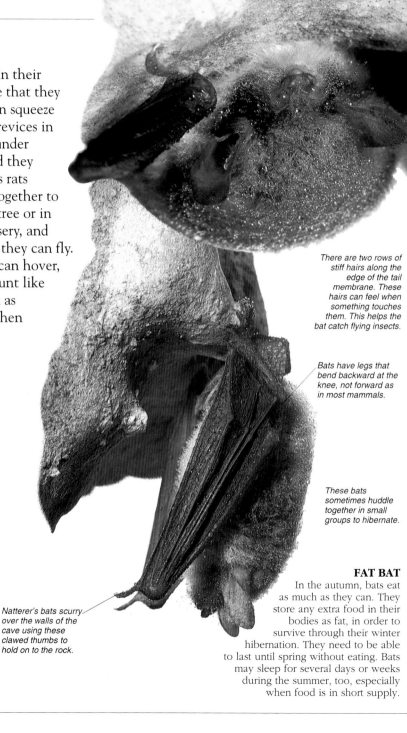

There are two rows of stiff hairs along the edge of the tail membrane. These hairs can feel when something touches them. This helps the bat catch flying insects.

Bats have legs that bend backward at the knee, not forward as in most mammals.

These bats sometimes huddle together in small groups to hibernate.

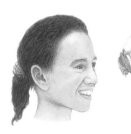

GUESS WHAT?
Bats do not hibernate throughout the winter, but wake up every few days or weeks. This allows them to move to the best part of the cave, depending on how cool and moist the air is.

CHOOSE A COOL CAVE
Bats are unusual among mammals, because their body temperature goes up and down. When a bat is asleep, its body temperature drops to the same as its surroundings. This means that the bat does not waste energy trying to keep warm. It is important that the bat chooses a suitable cave to hibernate in. The cooler the cave is, the longer the bat's stores of fat will last.

Natterer's bats scurry over the walls of the cave using these clawed thumbs to hold on to the rock.

FAT BAT
In the autumn, bats eat as much as they can. They store any extra food in their bodies as fat, in order to survive through their winter hibernation. They need to be able to last until spring without eating. Bats may sleep for several days or weeks during the summer, too, especially when food is in short supply.

Long, fluffy fur traps warm air close to the bat's body. This helps keep it at the right temperature.

When a bat hibernates in a very cool, damp cave, beads of moisture collect on its fur.

CLEANING FLUID

Bats keep themselves very clean, and spend much of their time washing and grooming their fur. Special glands on the head and wings produce a liquid that the bat uses to clean itself. It licks its wings to prevent them from drying out and to keep them supple for flying. It even risks falling, by hanging upside down from the ceiling of the cave by one foot so that it can lick the toes on its other foot.

The long ears point forward so that the bat can hear the ultrasounds when they bounce back from an object in its path.

Long, sensitive whiskers around the mouth help the bat feel for nearby insects or other bats in the dark cave.

Close up, you can just see the tiny eyes. Like most bats, Natterer's bats have quite good eyesight.

SEE-THROUGH SWIMMERS

IN THE COOL, DEEP WATERS of underground chalk caves, blind cave fish dart around in groups. Most of them cannot see at all, but even at high speeds they hardly ever bump into one another. Good eyesight would be useless to them in the blackness of a cave. These fish are related to piranhas, and like them, they have razor-sharp teeth. They are omnivores (animal and plant eaters), and feed hungrily on whatever they find drifting in the water. These fish are partly see-through because their skin has no color pigment. The pinkish color is caused by the blood inside their bodies. Like most other kinds of fish, the females lay eggs in the water. The fry (young) hatch out after only two or three days, and can swim well at about six days old.

GUESS WHAT?
When alarmed, blind cave fish produce a special substance from glands in their skin. This substance contains a chemical that frightens off other fish.

GOING, GOING, GONE
You can usually see the eyes of a young blind cave fish, but as the fish grows, its eyes get smaller. At about 13 days old, the eyes are covered with the first layer of skin. Gradually a layer of fat grows beneath the skin, and by about 52 days old, both eyes are completely hidden. Occasionally, a blind cave fish is born with good eyesight, which it keeps as it grows older. But some are born with no eyes at all.

Each eye is completely covered by a layer of skin and fat.

GOOD VIBRATIONS
Along each side of a fish's body there is a row of sense organs called the lateral line. It detects even the smallest vibrations in the water, and helps the fish feel its way around. This is why blind cave fish never crash as they swim along.

Two dorsal fins on the back balance the fish.

The pelvic fin keeps the fish upright in the water.

This row of large, dark scales along the fish's side is the lateral line.

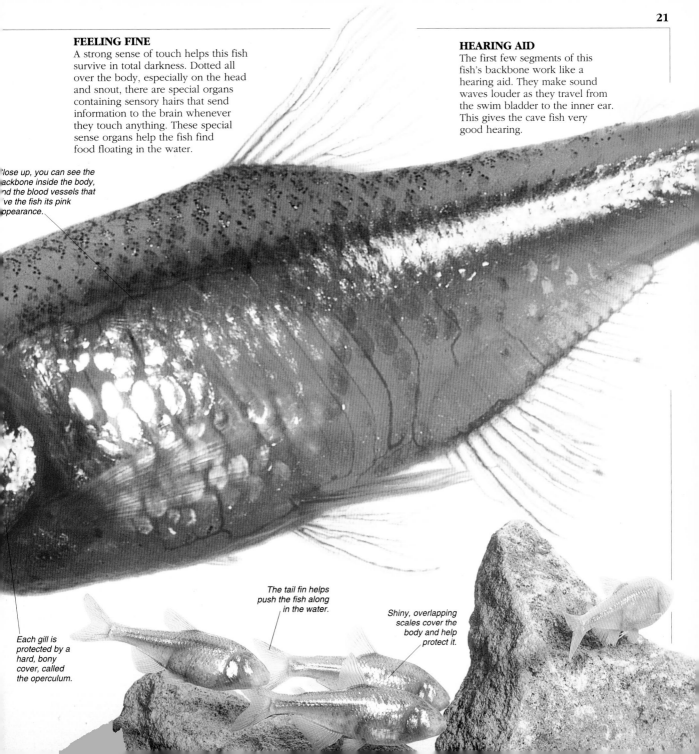

FEELING FINE

A strong sense of touch helps this fish survive in total darkness. Dotted all over the body, especially on the head and snout, there are special organs containing sensory hairs that send information to the brain whenever they touch anything. These special sense organs help the fish find food floating in the water.

HEARING AID

The first few segments of this fish's backbone work like a hearing aid. They make sound waves louder as they travel from the swim bladder to the inner ear. This gives the cave fish very good hearing.

Close up, you can see the backbone inside the body, and the blood vessels that give the fish its pink appearance.

Each gill is protected by a hard, bony cover, called the operculum.

The tail fin helps push the fish along in the water.

Shiny, overlapping scales cover the body and help protect it.

A CRY IN THE DARK

A BLOOD-CURDLING SCREECH echoing around a cave could well be the sound of a barn owl calling to its mate. In spring, barn owls form pairs for mating. The female usually lays between two and six white eggs in a hollow tree, a cave, an old barn, or on a cliff ledge. She sits on the eggs to keep them warm until they hatch, which takes about 30 days. The young owlets are covered with fluffy, gray down at first, and they cannot see. For the first few weeks, the female guards the young and the male brings them all food. After about eight weeks, the owlets begin to fly and feed themselves. A barn owl hunts mainly by night, and preys mostly on voles, shrews, mice, and frogs. It flies low over the ground, listening for small creatures moving below. As soon as it hears something, it swoops down and snatches it up without a sound.

GUESS WHAT?
Barn owls do not hoot, but they make all sorts of other noises, including shrieks, squawks, and hisses. Sometimes young owls even snore while they are waiting for food.

LOOKING GOOD
Owls keep their feathers clean and neat by nibbling and stroking them with their bills. This is called preening. Preening gets rid of dirt and parasites, such as feather lice and mites. Every so often, the bird presses its bill against a special gland under the tail to collect preening oil for wiping over its feathers. This oil keeps the feathers in good condition, and also helps kill harmful bacteria.

HEAD FIRST
As the owl grabs prey with its large, powerful feet, the victim often dies instantly. If not, the owl crushes the skull with its strong bill, then swallows the prey whole, head first. Owls cannot digest bones, feathers, or fur, so they cough up these remains in the form of hard, black, shiny pellets.

Male barn owls are slightly smaller than females, and have no dark spots on their chests.

A soft fringe along the edge of each wing feather allows air to flow over them easily and quietly during flight.

Sharp, hooked claws, called talons, grasp prey.

The female uses her hooked beak to tear up food for her young.

By breaking open a dry owl pellet like this one, you can figure out what the owl ate.

LIGHT AS A FEATHER
The owl's body is extremely small, and weighs only about 11 oz. But it has a thick covering of hundreds of soft, downy feathers. These make the bird's body look much bigger than it really is. The feathers also keep heat in, so the bird does not need to use up lots of energy trying to keep warm.

Each body feather is made up of thousands of little hairs called barbs. These hook together much like a zipper, making the feathers strong and waterproof.

This male owl has lowered his head to warn another owl that it has entered his territory.

FACE MASK
This owl's heart-shaped face is called the facial disc. The white feathers on the face are positioned so that they help direct sound into the ears on each side of the head. The owl has excellent hearing, but you cannot see its ear openings because they are hidden by feathers.

ON THE ROCKS

DEEP INSIDE THE CAVE, where no plants can grow, cave crickets feed on whatever they can find. These long-legged insects are scavengers, eating all kinds of plant and animal remains, including things that drift or float into the cave. This is why they can survive so far away from the outside world. The temperature and the amount of food in the cave do not change much from season to season, so these crickets can breed all year round. Male crickets use a special call to attract females for mating. After mating, each female lays her eggs in the earth on the floor of the cave. About a month later, the eggs hatch into young, wingless crickets called nymphs. They look like smaller versions of their parents. Every few weeks the nymphs molt (shed) their skin, growing larger each time. After about five molts, they are fully grown, and ready to mate and lay eggs of their own.

SINGING IN THE DARK
Adult male crickets make a special mating sound. They also sing, or chirp, to warn rival males to stay away. They make these chirping sounds by rubbing their wings together. When many crickets are singing at the same time, they can make a lot of noise.

Sharp spikes and spines cover the lower part of each back leg.

This female's tiny wing buds will never develop into wings. Only male cave crickets have wings.

GUESS WHAT?
Cave crickets are also known as camel crickets because they have humped backs, just like camels.

Tiny hooks on each foot help the cricket cling to the walls of the cave. The hooks work so well that the cricket can hang upside down.

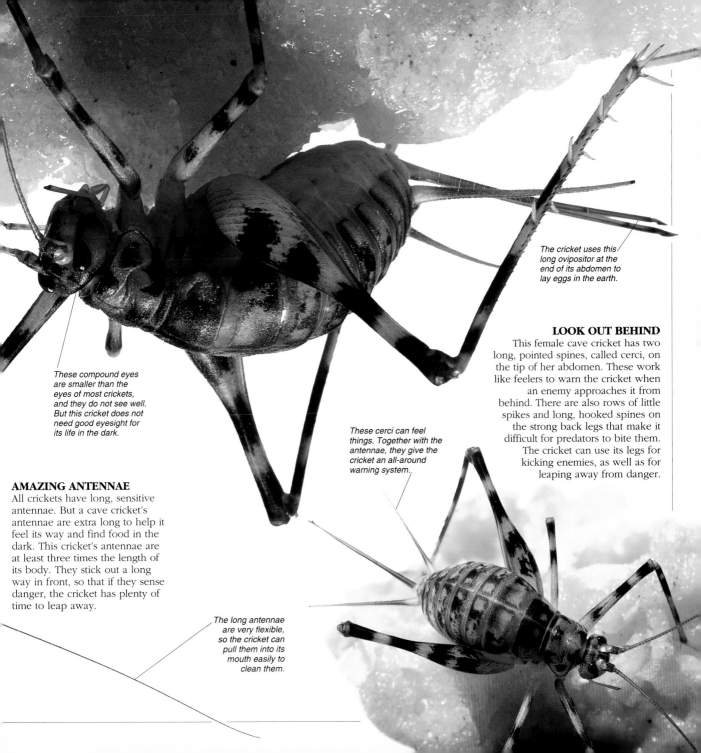

The cricket uses this long ovipositor at the end of its abdomen to lay eggs in the earth.

LOOK OUT BEHIND
This female cave cricket has two long, pointed spines, called cerci, on the tip of her abdomen. These work like feelers to warn the cricket when an enemy approaches it from behind. There are also rows of little spikes and long, hooked spines on the strong back legs that make it difficult for predators to bite them. The cricket can use its legs for kicking enemies, as well as for leaping away from danger.

These compound eyes are smaller than the eyes of most crickets, and they do not see well. But this cricket does not need good eyesight for its life in the dark.

These cerci can feel things. Together with the antennae, they give the cricket an all-around warning system.

AMAZING ANTENNAE
All crickets have long, sensitive antennae. But a cave cricket's antennae are extra long to help it feel its way and find food in the dark. This cricket's antennae are at least three times the length of its body. They stick out a long way in front, so that if they sense danger, the cricket has plenty of time to leap away.

The long antennae are very flexible, so the cricket can pull them into its mouth easily to clean them.

SCRAP COLLECTORS

COCKROACHES LIKE DARK, damp places best, so a cave makes a perfect home. These shiny, brown insects look like beetles, but they are more closely related to praying mantises and termites. Surinam cockroaches burrow in the floor of the cave and scuttle about on the walls, searching for plant and animal remains to eat. They feed on almost anything they can find, including dead bats, bat droppings (guano), and fungi. A female cockroach may start to lay eggs only a week after she has become a fully grown adult. Once the eggs have hatched, the young hide beneath their mother's body for safety. The female takes care of them until they are large enough to fend for themselves. Cockroaches take four to seven months to grow into adults, depending on the temperature inside the cave.

The body is protected by a hard, segmented exoskeleton.

This young cockroach has not grown its wings yet.

LITTLE ROACH
When a cockroach nymph hatches and leaves the egg case, it is soft and white. But its exoskeleton soon hardens in the air, and turns reddish brown. A young roach has no wings at first, and it looks much like a shiny, brown wood louse. As the nymph grows, it molts (sheds) its exoskeleton several times. The wings will be fully developed after the final molt.

GUESS WHAT?
Cockroaches have existed for more than 320 million years. During this time, their body shape and behavior have hardly changed at all. This shows how well they are suited to life on Earth.

Even young cockroaches have long antennae to help them find their way around in the dark.

The cockroach's flat body shape allows it to scurry into tiny crevices in the rock when danger threatens.

Wing cases protect the wings when they are not in use.

This shieldlike covering is called the pronotum. It covers the first segment of the thorax (the middle part of the body).

These two cerci are sensitive to vibrations.

A cockroach's legs may look quite short for the size of its body, but it can run very fast indeed.

The two antennae are long, flexible, and very sensitive.

A CASE OF EGGS
After mating, a female cockroach produces a special egg case called an ootheca. This is shaped like a little purse, and is attached to the cockroach's abdomen. The ootheca usually contains about 70 eggs, which are kept inside for about a week, until the larvae are ready to hatch.

RUNNING FOR COVER
Cave cockroaches can sense vibrations in air and in the ground. They detect minute movements with their antennae, and with the hairs on the taillike cerci, at the tip of the abdomen. A cockroach can often sense an enemy long before it gets close enough to attack, so it has plenty of time to run and hide.

A FRINGE OF FERNS

LIKE ALL GREEN PLANTS, ferns need sunlight to produce their food. They cannot grow in the darkness of a cave, but you will often see a fringe of green leaves around the entrance. Ferns are simple plants. They have roots, stems, and leaves called fronds, but no flowers, so they cannot produce seeds. Instead, they produce microscopic specks, called spores, like mushrooms. The life cycle of a fern has two stages. First the adult plant produces spores, which are carried on the breeze. If a spore lands in moist soil, it develops into a tiny, heart-shaped plant, called a prothallus. This has hairlike roots on the underside that take in water and nutrients from the soil. Each prothallus produces male and female cells, called gametes. Once a female gamete has been fertilized by a male gamete, it forms a zygote. This grows into a new, full-sized fern plant, and the whole cycle starts again.

SPORE STORE
On the underside of a frond there are groups of spore-producing structures, called sporangia. When the conditions are right, the sporangia split open to release a dusty cloud of microscopic spores into the air. Each of these tiny spores could eventually develop into a new prothallus.

Inside the stems of this sea spleenwort there are special tubes. These tubes carry water and minerals up to the fronds, and help to keep the stems from drooping.

These brown patches are called sori. Each one is a group of tiny sporangia.

A WATERPROOF COAT
Ferns have a waterproof covering on their fronds that prevents them from drying up. In most ferns, like this maidenhair fern, the fronds are divided into leaflets, called pinnae. Each pinna is made up of tiny leaflets called pinnules. But in some ferns, such as the hart's tongue fern, the fronds are joined like a single leaf.

The undivided fronds of this hart's tongue fern look more like the leaves of a flowering plant.

Mosses, like ferns, are very simple plants. Most of them use their leaves to take in moisture from the air. They also have rootlets to cling on to rocks or soil.

GUESS WHAT?
Ferns have existed for more than 300 million years, so they are among the oldest plants on Earth. In certain tropical forests some kinds of ferns grow up to 75 ft. tall. These huge plants are known as tree ferns.

The tiny leaflets on each pinna are called pinnules.

The green color in these leaves is chlorophyll.

GLOSSARY

Abdomen *the rear part of the body*
Antennae *a pair of feelers*
Bacteria *microscopic plant organisms*
Cerci *taillike feelers at the tip of the abdomen in animals, such as insects*
Chitin *the strong substance that makes up an animal's exoskeleton*
Chlorophyll *the green pigment in plants, which they use for photosynthesis*
Compound eyes *eyes that consist of many separate lenses*
Echolocation *the use of reflected sound to locate an object*
Exoskeleton *a tough covering on the body, made of chitin*
Gamete *a male or female sex cell*
Hibernate *to rest or sleep during the cold months of the year*
Larva *the young, grublike stage of an animal, such as an insect*
Lateral line *the line of sense organs along each side of a fish's body*
Molt *to shed the skin or exoskeleton*
Nocturnal *active at night*
Nymph *the larva of certain kinds of insects, such as crickets*

Ootheca *an egg case that certain kinds of insects, such as cockroaches, produce*
Operculum *a protective cover, such as a fish's gill cover*
Ovipositor *the egg-laying tube at the tip of the abdomen in most female insects*
Pheromone *a chemical produced by some animals that affects the behavior of others of the same kind*
Preen *to tidy and clean the feathers*
Pronotum *the protective cover over the first segment of an insect's thorax*
Roost *a place where animals rest or sleep, often high up*
Spores *seedlike bodies produced by many plants and simple animals when the male and female sex cells pair*
Thorax *the front part of the body, containing the heart and lungs*
Ultrasounds *sounds that are too high for a human to hear*
Venomous *poisonous*
Vibrations *tiny movements in air, in water, or underground*
Zygote *a fertilized egg cell, which will eventually develop into a new life*

CAVE LIFE

TREES
of
MICHIGAN
Including Tall Shrubs

Linda Kershaw

with contributions by

Anton A. Reznicek & Bill Cook

LONE
PINE

Lone Pine Publishing International

Distributed by Lone Pine Publishing
1808 B Street NW, Suite 140
Auburn, WA, USA 98001

Website: www.lonepinepublishing.com

Library and Archives Canada Cataloguing in Publication

Kershaw, Linda J., 1951–

Trees of Michigan, including tall shrubs / Linda Kershaw.

Includes bibliographical references and index.
ISBN-13: 978-976-8200-07-5
ISBN-10: 976-8200-07-3

1. Trees—Michigan—Identification. 2. Shrubs—Michigan—Identification.
I. Title.

QK167.K47 2006   582.1609774   C2006-901651-8

Technical Review: Anton A. Reznicek, Bill Cook
Separations & Film: Elite Lithographers Co.

Cover photo by Hans Blohm/Masterfile

The photographs in this book are reproduced with the generous permission of their copyright holders. A full list of photo credits appears on p. 6, which constitutes an extension of this copyright page.

Disclaimer: This guide is not intended to be a "how to" reference guide for food or medicinal uses of plants. We do not recommend experimentation by readers, and we caution that a number of woody plants in Michigan, including some used traditionally as medicines, are poisonous and harmful.

PC: 13